CRISPY SQUIRREL
AND VIMTO TRIFLE

Fifty great recipes from the extraordinary
culinary adventures of award-winning chef

ROBERT OWEN BROWN

MCR BOOKS

www.mcrbooks.co.uk

First published 2013 in England by Manchester Books Limited
Manchester Books Limited,
2 Pennyblack Court, 2a Barton Road,
Worsley, Manchester. M28 2PD

Text copyright © Robert Owen Brown
Additional text and editing by Neil Sowerby

Photography copyright © Joby Catto

Design by Anti Limited
www.anti-limited.com

A CIP catalogue record for this book is available from the British Library.

ISBN: 978-0-9927590-0-1

Printed and bound by Buxton Press.

Manchester Books Limited
www.mcrbooks.co.uk

To Arran
Just so you know what your Dad's been up to.
Too much rock for one hand.

And Vader's steady hand and huge heart.

CONTENTS

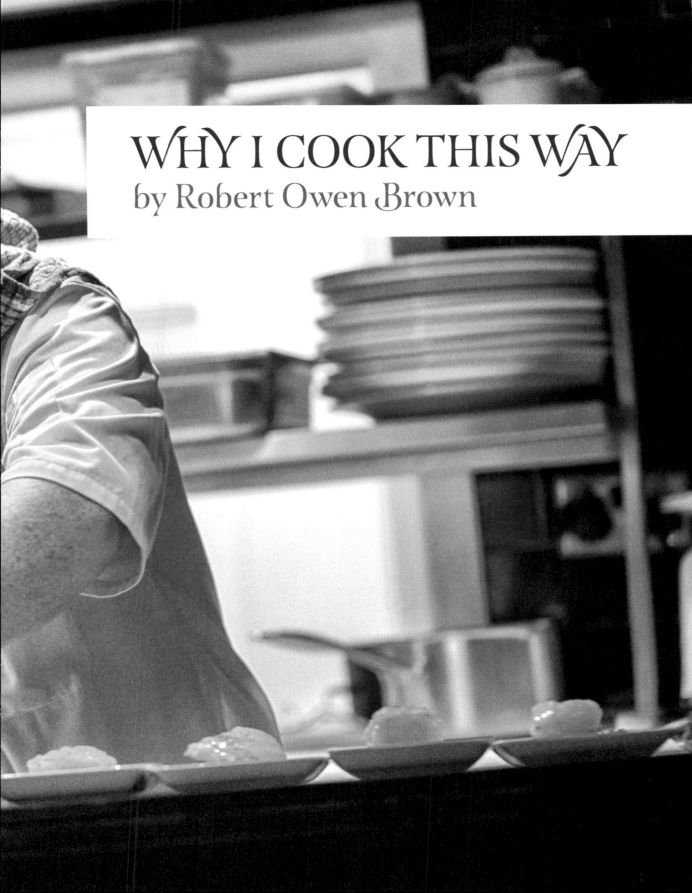

WHY I COOK THIS WAY
by Robert Owen Brown

Four words sum up my food philosophy:

Honest. Regional. Seasonal. Fresh.

Essential to all this are the small suppliers. The girls and guys who say *"Hi, Rob"* on the phone because they know my voice. Not *"Good afternoon, this is such and such, can I have your account number please?"*

Mine are the kind of **honest** contacts who will spot something in the market and call you, knowing you're going to want, need or just love it.

The sort of folk who grow/forage/catch/supply just what you require. Take Wayne the Butcher, from Styal Meats. The sort of bloke you can phone at three in the afternoon to order 10lb of tripe and he'll leave the golf course to get it for you. Like me, he gets excited about hunting out both the greatest cuts of meat and the squidgiest bits of offal. He's a mentor, a shoulder to cry on, an arse-kicker. You don't get that kind of service at a supermarket counter.

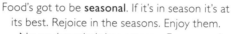

Food's got to be **seasonal**. If it's in season it's at its best. Rejoice in the seasons. Enjoy them. Never deny their importance. For example, don't eat a strawberry in December. Tease yourself. Hold on and wait for the locally grown ones at the height of summer. They are going to be ten times better.

The **fresh** stuff doesn't have to go to waste either. This is where the old (and new) preserving methods come in.

I use rapeseed oil instead of olive oil because it is British and sustainable. It is also delicious and better to fry with. Lard for pastry and suet for puddings suits me just fine. Tomatoes I hardly touch because, alas, home-produced aren't as good as Southern Europe's. My fish is from home waters, so exotics are out.

In the Mark Addy we serve wines from across the world because it would be daft not to in a restaurant, but we also have a choice of six cask beers, all from our brilliant local breweries. I'd recommend matching the different styles to different dishes.

I cook **regionally** because we have a wealth of amazing produce in the North West – fantastic fish and shellfish, world class game, dairy and meat. Why would I want to cook with anything else?

Why would I need to?

Old-fashioned? No. Authentic? Yes. But not rigid. Some of my dishes are steeped in history and true to their roots. Some of my food has been kicked up the arse all the way into the 21st century.

Food should taste of what it is. I like it to look like what it is as well.

The great chef, Fergus Henderson, had a profound effect on me too. I consider myself his disciple in the North. He gave me confidence to revisit the offals of my childhood and turn them into tasty, appealing dishes that are relevant today.

Lurking behind all this "nose to tail eating" is a deep belief that if you are going to take a creature's life you have a moral responsibility to use all of it. I believe we should enjoy the offal for what it is, not mince it up and hide it away.

I was flattered to be labelled "Champion of the North" by one critic. Not because I'm easily flattered, but because what we have; what I choose to cook; is worth championing.

Manchester, Salford and all the proud towns around are not Paris, not Naples, not Texas. Enjoy brasserie cuisine, pizza and pasta, ribs and burgers, but let's not neglect our own culinary treasures.

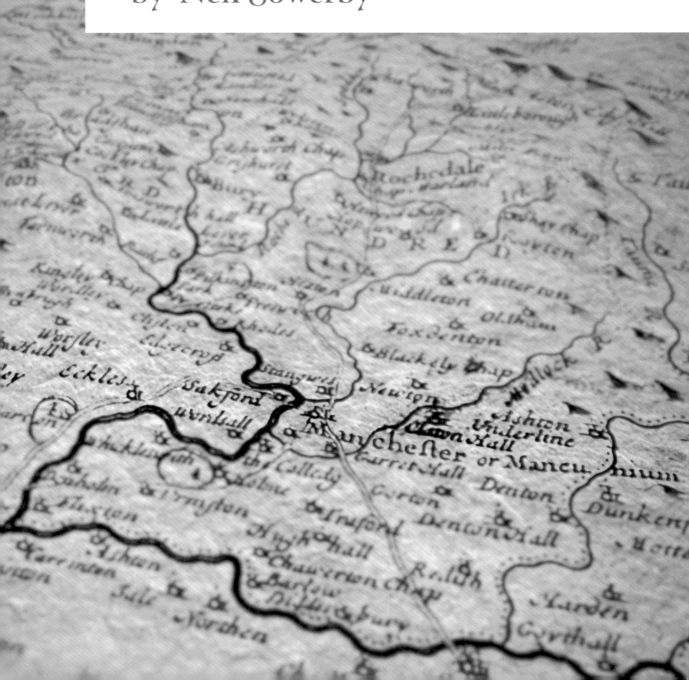

INTRODUCTION
by Neil Sowerby

This is a book about a chef, a very special chef. It's also about a river. Their destinies are intertwined. As a boy, Robert Owen Brown roamed the wild garlic-rich upper reaches of the Irwell. As a man, he cooks on its banks in the city, on the Salford side but with a view across to big brother Manchester. On matchdays boats leave his dining pub, the Mark Addy, for Old Trafford, ferrying fans fed and watered. It's a winner.

Rob's own horizons stretch further, much further – right down the Ship Canal, into which the Irwell flows, and out to the Irish Sea. Fish is never as fresh as the stuff you catch yourself and this is a cook as handy in a chartered fishing boat off the Mersey Estuary or North Wales as he is shooting game inland. Foraging and sourcing the very best ingredients also come naturally to this generous kitchen spirit, whose cooking is rooted in the north west soil and its industrial heritage.

The end product on the plate has garnered countless accolades in recent times when Rob has finally settled down in a kitchen he can truly call his own. OK, it's not the biggest, crammed under the final brick arch of this odd architectural blend of Industrial Revolution cellar and Seventies riverside disco. Cuts and burns are commonplace as his young team jostle for space, but there is a sense of harmony here. Front of house, too. All down to the captain at the helm, the one with the ginger curls and beard, who always totes two spoons for luck. Chefs are a superstitious breed.

RABBIT SURPRISE

"The bunny rabbit staring up at me with sad eyes is unlike any I've seen before. It has been skinned and is sitting, still whole, in a broth. The baguette I'm clutching is another new experience. I am 13. In the Dordogne. On a school exchange. Hardly been beyond Bury before. My French is limited to *Oui* and *Non*. I can hardly say *Non* to my first meal with the kindly French family hosting me. So I dip my bread. And like what I taste. Broth and rabbit flesh. Back home, I buy two rabbit legs on Bury Market. Take them home and grill them. To my parent's chagrin (another French word none of us knew). The result is tough as old clogs. But my career as a chef has begun."

Historically this is a dangerous spot. The Mark Addy, by the Albert Bridge, is named after a Victorian hero forever plunging into the fetid Irwell to rescue drowning folk. The pub has rescued Rob, in a way. It's been a career changer for someone lazy journalists once tagged "maverick chef".

Before the Addy, peripatetic was the word. Good career choices, odd ones, bad ones – but it was never dull. Even today our man chooses to live on a barge as if terra firma can only hold his swashbuckling gusto for so long. If this sounds one part pirate, one part gypsy, well that all contributes to the legend. An unengineered legend cocking a snook at the interminable celebrity chef bandwagon. Yet he is no recluse. Far from it.

At his best, Rob is an intuitive, off the cuff cook. Give him an audience at a cooking demo and the interaction is instant. This fundamentally shy man blooms, gives his time, shares his secrets. It's one of the people cooking the people's food. The recipes in this book reflect this. They don't shout at you. I'm always taken by his sheer politeness. I've known Rob for more years than I care to remember and I'm never Neil. Always "Mr Sowerby, sir". If I pop into the Mark Addy, while we are sharing a pint or two, a razor clam or a tranche of bone marrow with parsley sauce will appear at our elbow. I don't think it's special treatment for me, just part of the instinctive generosity I associate with him.

I said off the cuff. Well, give him a spit to roast a large carcass and he's a happy man. The odd bits left over, the innards and offal, a florid pig's head… Chef will turn them into a tasty treat, too. It's hardly molecular gastronomy, but it's also not Ye Olde Heritage Fayre. Rob may be steeped in the old cookbooks of Elizabeth Raffald and Eliza Acton and yoked to traditional kitchen practices, but his culinary skills were honed in classical hotel kitchens.

His apprenticeship in a school of hard knocks, which makes Masterchef look like a picnic, is a fascinating tale. It's not as if there's a family cooking tradition. Both his mother and sister are fine bakers, but it stops there. Fate had other plans for the boy of the family.

Rob was born in Stockport in 1969. His father was a driver in the newspaper industry, his mother a legal secretary. The family lived in Moss Side for a while, but then moved to Radcliffe. The hamlet in the Irwell Valley dates back to the Domesday Book. In the 19th century local coal powered the cotton mills, the river supplied water and it grew rapidly, but amid all that industry patches of attractive countryside clung on. They were Rob's rural refuge from school, where academically he didn't shine.

THE BEST USE FOR A FILING CABINET

Ingredients

Two turkeys, stuffed and wrapped in bacon

Method

Office equipment, heated to 200°C.

Christmas 2008. The Angel pub, Rochdale Road. Rob is chef. An 80-strong works party is imminent. Their boss wants to show them his knife skills by carving the festive fowl. Rob was 18 when he first cooked for this man. He even learnt his recipe for Caesar dressing off him. He can't let him down. But the turkeys, two 26kg beauties, are far too big for the oven. Meltdown looms. Rob, fag in hand, is forlornly leaning on his metal accounts cabinet, when… Eureka!

He ditches the paperwork and hauls the cabinet into the car park. Holes are drilled in the cabinet's side, a fire is lit in the bottom drawer space, then the turkeys are crammed in the top two drawers. A cash card sign "borrowed" from the local corner shop acts as a fire door and away they go. Three and a half hours later roast Christmas dinner is served. With all the trimmings.

In Domestic Science classes it was another matter. A teacher saw the promise and encouraged him. He prospered. A school exchange with Bury's twin town of Angouleme in the Dordogne did more. At the age of 13, he was introduced to the French devotion to their stomachs. You picked mushrooms in the woods to carry home to the kitchen. When you went fishing you didn't throw the catch back, you cooked it. Seaside wasn't for lazing about on the sand – you clawed oysters off the rocks and ate them. "Everything was reduced to live to eat, not eat to live… it made connections I never forgot," Rob recalls.

At 16, after an inspiring visit to his school by one of the tutors, he enrolled on a two-year course at Bury Catering College. In his spare hours he was already washing up at the Village Kitchen eaterie, the freckled lad in the unfortunate brown dungarees. But he soon moved up to commis chef at the Village Squash Club, learning to enhance every dish with a shot of monosodium glutamate. Different times.

A classier billet was the Chester Grosvenor, staying in digs for a training stint. Even that didn't prepare him for the savage challenge of his first job proper – in the kitchens

ESCALOPE OF BEER MAT

"Take one fine dining restaurant, one crazy, talented, off the wall chef, a team of disbelieving apprentices and me. Oh and one of those large beer mats Grolsch used to produce. Waiter tells the customer there is no veal left. It's the last table on a busy Saturday. Customer demands the veal. Waiter tells the chef. Chef says there is no veal. Waiter tells the customer. Customer reminds the restaurant manager and hotel manager what an important customer he is (ie rich). Restaurant manager and general manager remind the chef how important the customer is and how unimportant he is. Deathly hush. Sly smile from the chef and the check for one veal is called out to the kitchen. This young apprentice on the larder section looks confused. Chef smiles and disappears for five minutes. He comes back with a beer mat. He soaks it in the blood on the meat tray, breadcrumbs it, cooks it, serves it. To the important customer's immense satisfaction. He orders Champagne and distributes it among the kitchen brigade."

of Manchester's legendary Midland Hotel. The head chef ran a fanatical regime in pursuit of perfection. Rob could handle the sapping 70-hour week and what other professions would call bullying, because he understood how privileged he was to get this level of training.

ANTONIO MANCINI
THE MIDLAND MAESTRO

"An amazing Italian, head chef in The French Restaurant, whose teaching still resounds in my head. A man who would break an egg on the pass (the place where food is checked before leaving the kitchen to be served), so it cooked. Then he'd jump on the pass and do press-ups. The most macho man me and my commis had ever met. He would drop kick the door shut, charm waitresses, fight waiters, teach us knife drill and then how to sword fight. He played Spanish guitar at the end of a shift and sang constantly. He would set up a cheese trolley for the restaurant, tell you what each one was, the history, everything. At the end of the night he would test you on them. If you got any wrong, you ate the lot until you were sick. He scared you, changed you, led you. But, above all of that, he taught you.

"I once remember watching him bone a haunch of venison, it was slightly frozen. He slipped with the knife, the blade went straight into his gut. His response to the other senior chefs' concern over the growing puddle of blood was 'pack me off to housekeeping for a sewing kit'. Oh, and the man could cook."

But elsewhere the worms turned. In one of the large chain hotels Rob worked in during his early years, this level of intimidation finally sparked a mutiny – and a murder plot. The place was fully booked for an annual conference. Forty-two chefs, seven days of 600 covers at breakfast, lunch and dinner, culminating in a massive Phantom of the Opera dinner on the last night. A real mind-blowing dinner. Dry ice, orchestra, petit fours, ice sculptures, the works. Real pressure on the Head Chef (or the "Old Man").

Rob winces as he recalls: "End of the evening just as the petit fours are served. We are all elated. The Old Man appears from the office a little worse for wear. He bitches, moans and bollocks us. The team retire to the rest room for a staff beer feeling totally deflated. The senior sous chefs and the chef de parties start to talk of a mutiny. As the beer flows, this talk turns to murder. A plot is formed and an assassin chosen. A lad called Harry the Spider. It will be an accident. Every night the Head Chef would tour around all the walk-in fridges and freezers, checking stock. Harry was to wait until he went into the slippy, over-stocked freezer, push a shelf of stock on him, quickly get out and lock him in with the security chains. That evening for the first time in two years the Old Man didn't do a stocktake. He left early. Lucky escape for him and us. He always said he knew what was going on in his kitchen, even when he wasn't there."

The kitchens where Rob toiled in the Nineties and Noughties read like a roll call of Manchester's finest and quirkiest – Brasserie St Pierre, Lounge Ten, the Chop Houses and, most memorably, Reform at the top of Spring Gardens. Today, the former Reform Club first-floor premises house the ultra-reliable Room, but back in 1998 when it first opened as a restaurant/bar it seemed astonishingly decadent. Vast velvet drapes spooling across the floor, chandeliers, grotesque paintings, hand-cast brash ashtrays and salt and pepper pots (all nicked within a fortnight of opening). Oh, and they spent £120,000 on the kitchen… and considerably less on hiring Robert Owen Brown.

His own words capture it most vividly: "A brigade of chefs that gave me their all, hard working, aggressive, caffeine-fuelled monsters. Each with their own demons, all dancing to the beat of my drum. Waiting staff? Girls in high heels and mini-dresses so tight and short that serving food decently was almost impossible. A client base of footballers, movie stars, gangsters

UNHOLY COW AT GORTON MONASTERY

"A big Manchester event company gives me the opportunity to do the food for the opening of Gorton Monastery as a venue. It is to be, appropriately, a monastic type feast. Poached carp, rabbit pudding, hunks of bread.

"Centrepiece is a whole spit-roast Dexter cow, to be carried on a stretcher into the room in front of the guests. Easy! I go to the local blacksmith and have him construct a spit. Clamps either end and on the sides to hold the animal in place. Off to the farm to pick up the beast. The plan is to mount the animal on the spit at the farm, load it in the van and take it straight to the fire. So we somehow haul the 350kg cow onto the bar, go to lift it up and the bar bends. At 1am the farmer is cutting and welding scaffolding bars together.

"Time is tight, but we pull through. By 7am the beast is on the fire in Gorton. By 7pm three chefs with arc eye and three farmers carry in the sizzling whole animal. Yes, I had prayed."

and their entourage. A Spice Girl ordering poached fish and steamed vegetables with a jug of aged balsamic to pour over it; she was on a diet. When she ordered two crème brulees she wasn't. Then there were others who just came to stare. Champagne was delivered and consumed by the pallet load.

"It was a place where I learned the power of the press. We sold caviar, a lot of caviar, touching 500g a week. I received a phone call one day asking about who was buying it. My response was 'footballers and gangsters and none of them care what they are eating.' It was live on Richard and Judy – oops. I also recall a very famous footballer in the kitchen toilet with two ladies of the night. The amazing, wonderful Reform. The beautiful love child of Francis and Bernard Carroll. Thirty espressos to get you up and through the day and three bottles of Rocheberg Chenin Blanc to get you back down again."

Of course, it couldn't last. It didn't last. There was precious little glamour for Rob cooking in a suburban Darwen hotel, at the Lord Nelson pub back by his beloved Irwell… and in his own Radcliffe restaurant. That project crashed. He admits to not being a good businessman and didn't learn the lesson when he took over The Bridge Tavern in Manchester city centre. Which was a shame. It closed one wet Sunday morning, the day Observer food critic, Jay Rayner, named it as one of the top 10 UK places for lunch.

By now Rob had linked the hearty regional dishes he had perfected at the Chop Houses to the "nose to tail eating" championed by his hero, Fergus Henderson (like Rayner a constant supporter of our man). His shooting and fishing side came to the fore during a random interlude as chef on the Isle of Arran. Poaching deer and checking 150 lobster creels on Lamlash Bay was Rob heaven.

After a frantic 18 months at The Angel pub on Rochdale Road, Rob was rescued by the offer from the new team behind the Mark Addy. They would take on the business burden. He would just cook. And how he has cooked, attracting a loyal following among a new generation of food lovers. You'll find them blogging their thoughts on the Addy's acclaimed Gourmet Nights, appreciating the questing spirit that accompanies his sense of place and past.

He looks to the future, too. He has been heavily involved in the 2013 Manchester International Festival's Biospheric Project, a groundbreaking urban gardening experiment in an old Salford printworks. These are times of thrift and growing your own, not wasting the lesser cuts, the undervalued fish. Celebrating their virtues, indeed. Just like we always did in the north and Rob does now.

The fascinating voyage that began upstream on the infant Irwell's bosky banks is far from over.

All the recipes in this book are
designed to feed four
(with good appetites, of course).

An occasional dish such as a
mutton stew or the brawn may offer
substantial seconds or
leftovers to enjoy!

No techniques involved are beyond
a dedicated amateur cook.

SHELLED & SCALED
Seafood fresh inspiration

Lobster

You've probably guessed already that professional cooking is not all glamour. At The Midland the chef would sometimes buy huge quantities of lobster for functions. Sometimes up to 600 at a time. You can't believe how many boxes that takes up – or what state you are in after prepping them. Your hands are cut to ribbons, you're standing in a puddle of lobster juice and brains, your apron's dripping with it and stacks of broken shellfish surround you.

Speed was the key in a busy kitchen. It was just a case of twisting the two big front claws off the creature, putting them in one box, pulling the tail off and dropping into a separate box, then shovelling the heads into a huge stock pan.

Next, on with the wellies and into the pan of lobster heads you went. It was bit like crushing grapes – crunch, crunch. The mush would be turned into a wonderful bisque. Chef used to bite the heads off the lobsters and then bully us to do the same.

For the two recipes below I suggest buying the lobsters ready cooked from a good fishmonger. They are a great way to get two dishes for the price of one and make the most of your lobster. If you choose to use prawns instead for salad and soup, Dublin Bay (langoustines) are best. Or you could mix and match lobster and prawns in either dish.

Lobster Salad

Ingredients

2 cooked and chilled lobsters, shelled and all meat removed

10 quail's eggs, boiled, shelled and halved

200g cooked, chilled fine beans

200g skinned and seeded tomatoes

Salt and pepper

300g cooked and chilled waxy potatoes

2tsp chopped chives

3tbsp of rapeseed oil

Good dash Tabasco

Half lemon, juiced

50g mustard cress (poor man's micro salad)

Method

Gently combine the lobster, new potatoes, beans. tomato, chives, cress and eggs.

Mix the Tabasco, oil and seasoning.

Dress the salad, mix and serve immediately.

Posh Lobster Soup

Ingredients

600g puff pastry

Shells from the 2 lobsters (or from 1kg prawns)

150g tomato puree

200g carrot, diced

1 onion, diced

2 bay leaves

Half a leek, diced

1 celery stick, diced

Salt and pepper

4tbsp rapeseed oil

200ml double cream

1500ml fish stock

50g plain flour

Method

Heat a heavy-bottomed saucepan and add the oil. Put the shells in and cook rapidly. You want the shells to brown slightly as this will give a richness and depth to the soup.

Add the flour and tomato puree, mix to coat the shells, then add the vegetables and bay leaves.

Pour in the stock, slowly mixing all the time. Cook gently for one and a half hours, stirring occasionally. Add the cream and pass through a fine sieve, season and chill.

Divide the pastry into four and roll out to a 3mm thickness.

Three quarter fill your high-sided bowls with the soup. Cover with the pastry lid, egg wash and bake at 180C/ gas 4 until the lid is brown and crisp. Make sure the pastry never touches the soup.

Hot-smoked Mackerel with Blue Cheese and Spinach

Mackerel is among my favourite seafood and, as with all oily fish, hot-smoking is a perfect way to enhance the flavour. Its flesh is rich in Omega-3, which protects heart and brain. The sight of a freshly caught, gleaming mackerel lifts the spirits, too. What dampens mine is the shock news that the North East Atlantic mackerel fishery has joined the three quarters of worldwide stocks that are either declining or being fished beyond a sustainable level.

The Marine Conservation Society has taken the species off its ethical "fish to eat" list because the catch is now "far in excess of what has been scientifically recommended".

And yet it only seems like yesterday that the likes of Hugh Fearnley-Whittingstall were campaigning to persuade people to switch from overfished cod to this cheaply priced "superfood".

The mackerel catch is worth £205 million annually to British fishermen, so there is still a substantial amount about. It would be a shame to reduce this fabulous fish to an occasional treat. But please do go for day-bought, line-caught mackerel. If you don't feel up to hot-smoking at home, this dish also works well with bought-in kippers.

For the blue cheese you could use Blacksticks, Shropshire Blue or perhaps the brilliant example from Cheshire dairy Burt's, which has just been named Producer of the Year 2013 at The Observer Food Monthly Awards.

Ingredients

8 small mackerel fillets, pin-boned

80g butter

Salt and pepper

250g leaf spinach

160g soft blue cheese, crumbled or diced

40g new potatoes, cooked and halved

Juice of half a lemon

1tbsp rapeseed oil

For the hot smoking, your own choice of herbs or wood chips, maybe even tea

Method

You are going to need a smoke box and some wood chippings. They are cheap to buy and good fun. Maybe a fishing rod, too! You can even use a deep tray with a cooling rack, covered in tinfoil.

Heat your smoke box until you have a good level of smoke. And don't forget to open your windows. Lay the fish on to the rack, skin side up, cover and place in a hot oven, 200C/gas mark 6, for five minutes. I like to brush my fillets with melted butter first.

Heat a heavy bottomed frying pan, add the the rapeseed oil and when it is hot brown the potatoes a little. Add the spinach and wilt, followed by the cheese and butter. Allow to melt and season carefully.

Toss, then build a pile on the plate. Top with the fish and serve.

Warm Buckling Salad with Horseradish Sauce

Buckling should be better known. It's the name of a cure for a hot-smoked herring that was developed last century when the fish were abundant around these shores. In truth, it was always the poor relation of the kipper.

Kippers are split and cold smoked; the buckling is hot smoked whole, gutted but the roe and milt are left in. It keeps its moisture and essential oiliness. With golden brown skin and pale pink, opaque flesh, it is sweeter and less aggressively smoky than the kipper. I love it — that's why I seek it out in its Norfolk heartland. Once upon a time when herring was a staple — as in Scandinavia still — you didn't have to travel so far afield. Diversifying soap magnate Lord Leverhulme built a curing factory in Fleetwood and shipped the fish down refrigerated from the Hebridean Isles he owned.

I pair the buckling with pungent, fresh horseradish — a terrific starter or light lunch.

Ingredients

2 whole buckling, boned and flaked

1 cucumber cut into ribbons using a peeler

6 radishes, finely sliced

2 little gem lettuce, finely chopped

Good handful of chunky croutons

4tbsp home-made horseradish sauce, see below

8 boiled quail's eggs, shelled

4 skinned, de-seeded and chopped tomatoes

4 finely chopped spring onions

A small bunch of chives, chopped

Pepper

Sea salt

For horseradish sauce:

100g freshly grated horseradish

1tsp sugar

2tsp white wine vinegar

Pinch of salt

Pinch of pepper

200g soured cream

Method

Make horseradish sauce first: Put all the above ingredients in a blender and give a good whizz.

For the salad: Toss the buckling, lettuce, cucumber, radish and spring onions together with the horseradish sauce. Arrange in a bowl.

Scatter with chives, croutons, shelled quail's eggs (they take two minutes to boil) and tomato and serve.

Crispy Razor Clams

It's great fun gathering razor clams. Hard work but rewarding. They are found in wet sand and are only exposed at very low ebb tides. You spot them just under the surface by the little spout of water. To encourage them to come up pour a little salt in the spout hole. Get a knife under and twist to gather them. But be quick or they'll burrow down to escape. Take care because their shells can be as sharp as their name suggests. Purists might argue they are best eaten straight from the shell with plain melted butter, but I like adding this Asian spice edge to these substantial molluscs. Serves two razor clams per person.

Ingredients

I beaten egg

4 large spring onions, very finely sliced

I clove garlic, peeled and finely chopped

100g chopped coriander

I red chilli, de-seeded and very finely chopped

8 sheets of spring roll pastry

Pinch sea salt

50g chopped mint

I litre vegetable oil

I lemon, quartered

8 large razor clams

Method

Heat the oil in a deep fat fryer or a large pan to 180C/ gas 4.

Heat a large saucepan of water with the lemon in it. When it hits a rolling boil drop the clams into it for one minute only. No more or they will end up tough. Plunge the clams into iced water to stop the cooking.

Once cold, remove the clams from the shells, clean, pat them dry and place in the fridge.

In a clean bowl combine the onion, garlic, salt, chilli and mint.

Lay out the sheets of spring roll pastry and lightly brush with the egg.

Place a line of the onion mix on to the pastry, top with a clam and roll tightly as you would for a spring roll, making sure to fold in the edges.

Deep fry quickly until golden brown. Serve immediately.

Octopus Stew with Yorkshire Chorizo

Yorkshire chorizo is made near Skipton. You can buy it from their own farm shop in the village of Airton. Like the Spanish original, this chorizo gets its distinctive smokiness and deep red colour from using smoked Spanish paprika. The pork here, though, is British.

I love the richness of this dish. Try serving it with a lovely garlicky saffron mayonnaise and some crusty bread. Such a fantastic one-pot dish saves on the washing-up, too, which is nice.

Ingredients

900g cleaned octopus, cut into 5cm chunks

2tbsp rapeseed oil

2 large chopped onions

2 cloves of finely chopped garlic

2 bay leaves

500g chorizo chopped into 5cm chunks

900g tomato flesh, peeled and deseeded

500ml fish stock

2tsp smoked paprika

2tbsp chopped coriander

2tbsp finely chopped parsley

Salt and pepper

200g tomato puree

100ml white wine

Method

Heat the oil in a heavy-bottomed saucepan. Add the onion, garlic, thyme, bay leaves and paprika. Cook until the onion is soft and slightly caramelised. Now add the white wine and reduce by half.

Add the chorizo, tomato, tomato puree, fish stock and octopus and cook gently, stirring occasionally until the octopus is tender, about two hours.

Add the coriander and parsley and serve straight away.

Crab with Leeks

Crab and leek is a lovely combination of complementary sweet flavours and flaky textures. This dish couldn't be simpler and you are tucking into a truly sustainable, affordable feast in its own solid packaging. The most common crab, the brown, is low in cholesterol and fat and rich in essential minerals such as zinc and selenium (said to be good for boosting a low sperm count, apparently). My only warning is on the purchasing. A reliable fishmonger will not fob you off with a soft crab that has recently shed its old shell. They may look shiny and attractive in their new casing but, as they strive to harden up, inside they are pumped up with water and boast precious little meat. Best go for the old, battered ones that have spent their time guzzling.

Ingredients

I crab weighing Ikg (get your fishmonger to extract the meat, retain the shell)

300ml double cream

Salt and pepper

Itsp English mustard

350g thinly sliced leeks

200g Cheddar cheese, grated

50g butter

Method

Heat a heavy saucepan, add the butter and sweat the leeks until soft, then add the double cream and reduce by half. Add the crab meat, mustard and half the cheese mixed together.

Heat thoroughly, season and place back into the cleaned shell. Sprinkle on the rest of the cheese and glaze under the grill.

Fillet of Sea Bass with Fennel

This is one of those cheffy dishes that are a bit tough to produce but not only does it look fantastic it tastes it as well. Try and buy wild fish, the larger the better, so you get a thick fillet. The wild fish is far superior to the farmed. Get the fishmonger to scale it for you or you'll be finding scales about for months. Bass deserves its renown, perfect for simple cooking, but its robust creamy flesh stands up to a variety of strong flavours – in this case assertive olives and fennel's aniseedy bite. The French call the fish "loup de mer" – sea wolf – because it is an aggressive predator. There's always a danger of over-fishing such a popular plateful, so there are stringent protective measures in place. It's hard to believe that sea bass was once regarded as a cheap alternative to cod, only becoming fashionwable in the Eighties (though the Chinese always prized it).

Ingredients

800g sea bass fillets

2 large bulbs fennel, shredded

4tbsp rapeseed oil

Pinch salt

Pinch pepper

1 lemon

30g peeled tomato, diced

Zest of 1 lemon

14 chervil sprigs

14 black olives

14 nicely shaped new potatoes
(peeled and cooked in saffron would be lovely)

50g unsalted butter

Method

Trim the top of the fennel bulbs, then remove the base, so they will stand up.

Gently remove any pin bones from the bass fillet, cut in to triangle shapes, aiming for three to a portion, then place the fish in the fridge.

Blanch the large pieces of fennel quickly in boiling, salted water, then set aside.

Heat two heavy frying pans with half the oil in each,

Place the fish in one pan, skin side down, making sure they don't touch each other. Cook until the skin is crispy and golden brown, then turn over and season.

Add the fennel to the other pan and cook rapidly for two minutes. Include the butter, lemon zest and juice, tomato and olives. Season to taste.

Once both the fennel and the fish are cooked start to build your dish, using as much artistic flair as you can muster.

Dab with Spring Onions and Bacon

I love these tasty, sweet little flat fish, but they're not very popular for some reason, often being discarded in a catch. Perhaps it's the size that puts folk off – they are fiddly to bone – but they are the equal of lemon sole. I source mine from Wales and Morecambe Bay and they are very inexpensive. One is good, but two is a feast. Cook them on the bone for a better taste.

Ingredients

8 small or 4 larger dabs, fins and head removed

200g bacon, cut in strips

1 garlic clove, crushed, chopped

50g unsalted butter

2tbsp rapeseed oil

Juice of 1 lemon

Salt and pepper

4tbsp chopped parsley

8 spring onions, finely chopped

200g flour

Method

Heat a large heavy bottomed frying pan and add the oil.

Lightly flour the dabs and cook on one side for three minutes until golden brown.

Turn over the fish, scatter the bacon and garlic around the fish and cook for two further minutes.

Add the lemon juice, butter and spring onions, then season and baste the fish. Cook for a further minute and serve.

Skate Wing with Capers and Butter

Skate is a delicious oddball fish. At the fishmonger's it is inevitably prepared in wing form. The fish's flat, diamond shape yields two "wings" – fan-shaped with a ribbed texture, the gelatinous pinky-white flesh clinging to cartilaginous bones. Traditional advice was to soak for 24 hours to rid it of its off-putting ammonia smell. And, yes, it is also fiddly to fork that flesh out (don't try and fillet it beforehand). Yet the rewards are great. Sharp, vinegary sauces are best for this fish – or the traditional "black butter". My variant uses capers to perk up the sauce. A rare treat.

Ingredients

2 small skate wings or one large wing cut in two, about 300g per person

2tsp rapeseed oil

4tbsp plain flour

½tsp paprika

100g unsalted butter

2tsp roughly chopped capers

2tsp chopped parsley

Salt and pepper

Method

You need a heavy bottomed frying pan big enough to accommodate both bits of fish with room to spare.

Combine the flour and paprika and lightly dust your skate wings.

Heat your oil in the pan, add your fish and colour to a golden brown on one side. Cook on a medium heat, not too fast – you want it only half cooked through before turning it over to cook for a further minute.

Add your butter and capers. Turn up the heat and continue cooking until the butter browns, basting constantly.

Season and serve with rich mashed potato.

FURR'D & FEATHER'D
Game: set and matched

Southern Fried Crispy Squirrel

You can buy squirrel online these days from eco-savvy operations like the Wild Meat Company in Suffolk. It's advisable to order it ready skinned (the tail is discarded). Still it is much cheaper to source your own locally from a mate with an air rifle or the more enlightened local butcher/game dealer. I get mine from Frost's of Chorlton, who usually has a few in the freezer. We are talking the common grey, not the endangered red, squirrel, of course. Their diet is basically nuts, so this is a healthy meat, albeit not a substantial one. Usually allow a whole squirrel per person.

This particular "Southern fried" recipe ekes out the raw material, giving it a tang in a recipe loosely adapted from Colonel Sanders' finest. Lovely with coleslaw and baked beans. This dish works equally well with rabbit.

Ingredients

3 squirrels, jointed

I small onion, chopped

300g panko (Japanese breadcrumbs)

I small carrot, chopped

2 beaten eggs

I stick of celery, chopped

2tsp of smoked paprika

Itbsp of rapeseed oil

Itsp of mustard powder

Pinch salt and pepper

250g butter

I litre chicken stock

200g plain flour

¼tsp celery salt

I bay leaf

Method

Heat the oil in a large heavy casserole pan.

Brown the squirrel then, add the vegetables, bay leaf, butter and stock. Simmer for 50 minutes – drain the stock and use for something else. Now cool the squirrel.

Combine the mustard, paprika and celery salt with the breadcrumbs.

Flour the squirrel, then dip in the egg, followed by the crumbs.

Deep fry at 160C/gas 3 until golden brown and crispy.

Finally, season and serve.

Wood Pigeon with Black Pudding and Elderberries

One of those symbiotic dishes – the pigeons get big and fat feeding on all the crops at the same time as the elderberries ripen. Of course, all that crop feeding doesn't please the farmers who, I'm sure, would be glad to see pigeon as a more everyday dish on the nation's plates! They are not, partly because of their vermin image and a perception they are rather muscly and tough from all that flying. Young, plump pigeons are fine for roasting but after that ingenuity must come in. The crown is the prime cut – the dense breast on the bone, which benefits here from the rich fruit sauce.

Ingredients

4 wood pigeon crowns (leg meat and undercarriage removed)

100g elderberries

20g redcurrant jelly

200g black pudding, skinned and diced

Salt and pepper

2tbsp rapeseed oil

60g butter

300g pigeon stock

For stock:

1 carrot

1 onion

1 leek

1 celery stick

1 litre cold water

1 bay leaf

6 peppercorns

Method

For the stock: In a heavy stockpot, brown the pigeon bones. Add the veg and brown that as well. Add the water, peppercorns and bay leaf and bring to the boil quickly. Once the stock has boiled turn it down to a gentle simmer. Skim any foam that appears and simmer for two and a half hours.

Strain through a fine sieve into a clean pan and reduce by three quarters. Set aside.

To cook the pigeon: Heat a heavy-bottomed, oven-proof pan. Add the oil and brown the pigeon all over, seasoning as you do.

Stand the pigeons in the pan with the wishbone down, then fill the breast cavities with half the butter.

Roast in the oven at 220C/gas 7 for 12 minutes. Remove and rest for five minutes in a warm place.

For the sauce: Bring the stock reduction to the boil. Reduce to a simmer, stir in the jelly and half of the elderberries. Cook for two minutes.

Strain the sauce, add the rest of the butter, the remaining elderberries and the black pudding. There are several fine North West producers. I'm usually torn between Chadwicks of Bury or The Real Lancashire Black Pudding Company of Haslingden. Stir until the butter dissolves. Spoon over the pigeons and serve immediately.

Roast Pheasant with Parsnips

Quintessentially English. A great use of one of our best game birds and one that is cheap as game chips. Served with bread sauce, watercress and parsnips (at their best during game season), it can't be beaten. Here bacon, redcurrant jelly and port provide the moistness that stops the game, low in fat, from getting too dry during the roasting process.

Ingredients

2 pheasants

8 strips of back bacon

Salt and pepper

4tbsp rapeseed oil

200ml Port or Madeira

2tsp redcurrant jelly

250ml game stock (preferably made from the game carcass, though chicken will do)

120g butter

2 sprigs thyme

2 small shallots, halved

6 large parsnips, peeled, split

Method

Stuff the pheasants with the shallot, butter and thyme.

Heat a heavy frying pan and brown the pheasants in a little oil, then remove.

Season the birds, then cover their breasts with the bacon strips.

Heat the remaining oil in a roasting tin and add the parsnips, then set the pheasants on top and roast at 200C/gas 6 for 30 minutes.

Remove pheasants and parsnips to a serving dish.

Drain any excess oil from the tray and place the tray on the hob until it is just smoking. Add the port, reducing by half and burning off the alcohol. Add the redcurrant jelly and stock and again, reduce by half. Season and pour over the pheasant.

Rabbits

Rabbit, it has to be wild. It's the quality of the wild stuff they eat which contributes to the flavour. Never buy frozen either – as you don't know where it's from. The rabbit really needs its fur on for you to gauge its age. Too long in the tooth and it's too tough. A good tip if you are buying pelt on is the bunny's ears. An old one, the lugs are like leather, while a youngster's snap like brittle paper. The presence of two rabbit dishes (there could have been more) shows how much I like this undervalued meat, once a staple of a rural and semi-rural, diet. There was me as a 13 year old in a shocking three quarter length fake Barbour hunting rabbits around the old Radcliffe brickworks. I was a pretty good shot with my air rifle, and used to take home a bagful. My mum and dad didn't eat rabbit. They thought I was a nutter. Maybe they were right.

Butter Cooked Rabbit with Mushrooms and Thyme

Ingredients

1 large rabbit, jointed or 4 good sized back legs

200ml dry white wine

600ml game stock or chicken stock

100ml double cream

Salt and pepper

2tsp finely chopped thyme

400g penny bun mushrooms or 200g dried mushrooms

1 onion, finely chopped

1 medium carrot, finely diced

1 bay leaf

1 crushed garlic clove

2tsp chopped parsley

150g butter

2tsp rapeseed oil

50g flour

Method

Heat the rapeseed oil in a heavy-bottomed frying pan.

Roll the rabbit in the flour to coat it evenly and brown in the oil.

Remove the rabbit. Add the vegetables, garlic and thyme. Cook gently until the onion is transparent.

Add the rabbit with 75g butter, wine and stock.

Cover, bring to the boil, skim, and turn down to a simmer for one hour or until the rabbit is soft. Remove the rabbit and keep warm.

Reduce the stock by half, add the cream and reduce by half again, stir in the remaining butter and pour over the rabbit. Serve.

Roasted Rabbit with Potatoes and Rosemary

Ingredients

1 rabbit, jointed
Coarse salt and finely ground pepper
1 clove garlic, finely chopped
Juice of 1 lemon
8 rosemary leaves
80ml rapeseed oil
16 small red-skinned potatoes

Method

Season the rabbit and place in a non-corrosive dish. Mix the garlic with the lemon juice, half the rosemary and half the rapeseed oil. Turn the rabbit in the marinade and leave in the fridge for several hours, turning occasionally.

Preheat the oven to 200C/gas 6. Place the rabbit pieces in a roasting pan and pour on the marinade. Cover the rabbit with a piece of foil. Toss the potatoes in the remaining oil, then sprinkle them with salt, pepper and the remaining rosemary leaves and place around the rabbit.

Roast for 20 minutes, then remove the foil from the rabbit. Roast for another 10 to 15 minutes until light brown and tender. If the rabbit seems to be drying out during cooking, add a little water or dry white wine.

Venison

These two recipes use different cuts of deer. It's hard to think of a healthier, more sustainable meat. And it's hardly an endangered species. In spring 2013 scientists called for a cull of 50 percent of the UK deer population, estimated at 1.5 million, more than since the last Ice Age and growing. The researchers from the University of East Anglia did suggest harvesting the animals for meat to make a cull ethically and economically acceptable. But are there too many Bambi lovers out there to make this viable? Certainly there's no point in buying inferior farmed when there's so much wild about and so many different breeds, each with their own distinctive taste.

A small Chinese Muntjac (I've seen them in Salford even) gives a quite different meat from a huge red stag that has gorged on heather. The first treatment is classic game cookery, but there's very much a local flavour to the second, which uses Bury brewery Deeply Vale's oatmeally DV8 stout to stew the venison with oatmeal dumplings. It seems right to sup a beer with it. Deeply Vale in the Pennine foothills hosted legendary festivals in

Venison Loin with Red Cabbage and Chocolate

Ingredients

400g venison loin

20g butter

140g red cabbage

Salt and pepper

30g dark chocolate

1 fondant potato (a disc of spud that has been baked in the oven in butter, thyme, garlic and chicken stock)

275ml venison stock reduction

Method

Make the venison stock in the way you would a beef stock but with the addition of one pig's trotter, cutting the cooking time down to six hours. You then need to reduce the stock by 75 per cent.

Heat the stock reduction with red cabbage in a small saucepan without a lid.

Place the fondant potato in the oven to warm on a small tray at 220C/gas 7 for 10 minutes.

Heat a heavy bottomed frying pan until very hot, add a splash of oil and seal the venison on all sides.

Place the venison on to the tray with the fondant potato for no more than five minutes. It has to be pink.

Add the chocolate and butter to the cabbage pan, mix well and remove from the heat. Remove the venison and potato from the oven, season and serve.

Venison Casserole with Stout

Ingredients

750g venison shoulder diced large

1 onion, finely chopped

1 clove garlic, crushed

2 litres stout

2tbsp golden syrup

1 large carrot, diced

1 stick celery, diced

50ml rapeseed oil

2tsp chopped thyme

50g flour

Salt and pepper

For the dumplings:

70g fine oatmeal

70g plain flour

1 heaped tbsp baking powder

1tsp salt

75g butter

5tbsp water

Method

Heat the oil in a heavy saucepan or casserole dish. Brown the meat in batches, add the diced vegetables, garlic and thyme before stirring in the flour. Add the stout slowly, stirring all the time, then the syrup. Simmer gently for two hours.

You could use any stout, even Guinness, but I prefer to support small local brewers and Deeply Vale's DV8 is just perfect.

Meanwhile make the dumplings by mixing all the ingredients together and forming into balls. Add the dumplings to the pot for the final 15 minutes and cover. Uncover, season to taste and serve.

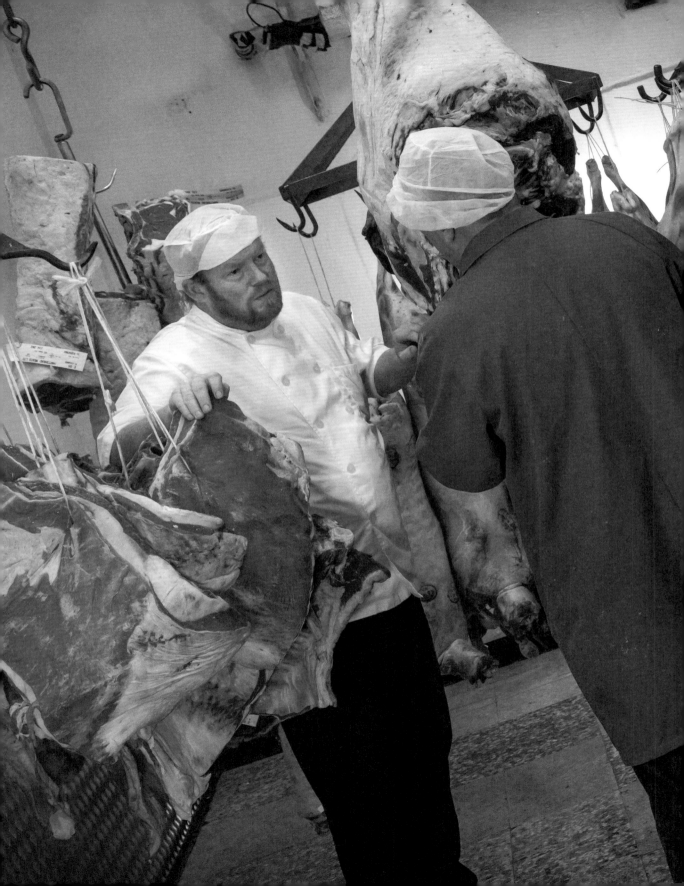

BIRD & BEAST
Roast, steamed and stewed

Roast Quail with Lavender

Elizabeth I, legend has it, insisted a jar of lavender preserve should be on the table for every meal. Since those times this beautiful, scented herb has usually been destined for the pot-pourri rather than the table. Which is a shame since it is a valuable culinary all-rounder in both sweet and savoury dishes. Our homegrown lavender, with its sweet herbal edge, akin to thyme and rosemary, may not be as pungent as its Mediterranean cousin, but it's still wise to use it sparingly. Fresh is best and that's what I'd recommend here. Quail is farmed, usually for its lovely speckled eggs, but it's got a dense gamey flavour once you've done the fiddly bit of levering the flesh off its tiny carcass.

Ingredients

8 whole quail

Small lemon, cut into eight

80g butter

4 garlic cloves, halved

3tsp fresh lavender

100ml chicken stock

100ml white wine

Salt and pepper

16 small new potatoes

16 small carrots, scrubbed

16 shallots, peeled

30ml rapeseed oil

Method

Heat the oven to 200C/gas 6.

Stuff each quail with half a garlic clove, a piece of lemon and a knob of butter, then truss them with a rubber band.

Heat a large oven proof frying pan and add the oil.

Brown the quail, then remove from the pan. Now lightly brown the shallot and potato.

Arrange the quail among the veg and sprinkle with the lavender. Place in the oven for 15 to 20 minutes. Remove and take the veg and quail from the pan. Drain any excess oil from the pan.

Add the white wine and reduce by half. Add the chicken stock and reduce again until your sauce is a lovely consistency.

Season and dress the quail and vegetables with the sauce.

Roast Dandelion and Burdock Duck with Damsons

*Damsons, purple and black skinned, were originally cultivated for dye production. The name Damson derives from the Latin **prunum damascunum**, "plum of Damascus". It is believed the fruit was first cultivated around the ancient city and introduced into England by the Romans. Remnants of damsons are often found during archaeological digs. Their old role has long been superseded by their culinary use in sweet and savoury dishes and, of course, in drinks such as damson gin or beer. The best are from the Lyth Valley in the Lake District – a true native fruit undergoing a revival. Here I roast them and marry their astringent flavour with the sticky, herbal sweetness of dandelion and burdock and some honey. It creates a perfect glaze for roast duck (domesticated not wild). Curly kale's a fine accompaniment.*

Ingredients

1 large duck

500ml dandelion and burdock (fizzy pop, or for something special dilute some of Fitzpatricks' cordial – Rawtenstall's finest)

300g damsons

Salt and pepper

3tbsp good honey

Method

Heat the oven to 220C/gas 7.

Place the duck and damsons in a deep roasting tin. Pour on the dandelion and burdock. Cover and roast for 1 hour.

Remove the cover and roast for a further 40 minutes.

Remove duck from tray and leave to rest.

Ladle the fat from the tray.

Strain the remaining liquid, forcing the damson pulp through the sieve.

Add the honey and reduce the sauce till it coats a spoon.

Glaze the duck and serve.

Mutton with Capers

It's now nigh on a decade since Prince Charles launched the Mutton Renaissance campaign – the object to promote "meat from a traceable farm assured sheep that is at least two years of age, has been finished on a forage based diet and matured for at least two weeks post slaughter". Thanks to such champions, it is now possible again to source this neglected treat.

We, of course, in the North West have long cherished the stuff… and hogget, young mutton slaughtered between one and two years of age. Most sheep are killed in their fourth or fifth month with the exception of a few spring-born lambs that are slaughtered in late autumn or winter – the true spring lamb. All very tasty, but properly hung mutton is something else. Try roasting it or braising it in the classic British combination below, where it turns out tender, silky and creamy.

Ingredients

1kg mutton shoulder, in chunks

2 large onions, diced

Black pepper

Salt

5tbsp capers

75g plain flour

75g butter

250ml double cream

1 litre brown stock (or substitute with a good shop-bought beef stock)

2tbsp rapeseed oil

Method

Heat a heavy bottomed pan or casserole dish. Add the rapeseed oil and brown the mutton pieces in it.

Sprinkle on the flour and mix to coat the mutton, then add the onion and stock.

Bring to the boil, reduce heat and simmer until the meat is tender.

Strain off the liquid and reduce by three quarters, reserving the mutton.

Add the double cream and capers. Reduce now until the sauce coats the back of a spoon. Stir in the butter and mutton. Season and serve.

Faggots (Savoury Ducks) with Red Onion Gravy

Old-fashioned, gutsy and honest, faggots are fabulous. I first met them at junior school. The dinner lady told me they were cat's brains. I believed her for a very long time. Tinned ones always made me laugh, same as meatballs which, of course, were kitten's brains. I laughed at the other kids getting excited about getting them for tea. I was one of the few who knew what they were really eating. You need a good traditional butcher to supply you the ingredients, in particular the lacy caul fat (a thin membrane which surrounds the internal organs of cows, sheep, and pigs). All very cheffy. If you can't get it don't worry, the dinner ladies didn't use it. Wrap them in flattened streaky bacon instead.

Ingredients

30g lard

2 medium onions, finely chopped

1tsp chopped fresh sage

1tsp thyme

2 cloves garlic, finely chopped

150g minced lamb or beef

150g minced ox kidney

150g minced heart (get your butcher to trim it first)

150g minced liver, pig's for preference

Salt and pepper

1 egg

50g breadcrumbs

500g caul fat

For the gravy:

3 large sliced red onions

1tbsp lard

550ml beef stock

300ml Guinness

1tsp chopped thyme

20g plain flour

20g caster sugar

Method

To make the gravy: Heat the lard in a heavy-bottomed pan, add the thyme, onions and sugar and cook until it all turns a lovely brown caramel colour.

Beat in the flour and then slowly add the beef stock, mixing all the time to avoid lumps. Now add the Guinness. Bring to the boil and then simmer gently for 10 minutes. Set aside.

To make the faggots: Combine all the ingredients apart from the caul fat and lard in a bowl and mix well.

Mould the faggot mix into a dozen 50g balls. Place them in the fridge for two hours.

Cut the caul fat, if you have it, into squares and wrap around the faggots.

Heat the lard until just smoking, then gently seal the faggots. Remove from the heat and pour the gravy over the faggots and bake at 200C/gas 6 for 15 minutes. Baste the faggots with the re-heated gravy and serve.

Hand-raised Chicken and Mushroom Pie

This is a dish I've often used to get kids involved in cooking – because it is literally so hands on. A bit like play dough. Hand-raised (or hot water) pastry is a British speciality, normally used to make a pork or game pie. Originally, it was only the filling that was eaten, the crust container was merely there to seal in the juices and prevent the meat filling from drying out. What a waste.

Ingredients

500kg cooked field mushrooms, sliced

1kg chicken breast, finely chopped

2 eggs, one for filling, one for pastry

500g lard

750g plain flour

150g water

1 onion, finely chopped and fried

Salt and pepper

Method

For the filling: Combine chicken, onion, mushroom, egg, seasoning and butter and place the mix in the fridge. Or for a classy touch, keep the mushrooms separate so you can layer them in, as in the photo.

For the pastry: Put the water, lard, salt and pepper into a pan and heat until the lard has melted. Immediately remove from the heat, add the flour and egg and beat rapidly until smooth. Allow the pastry to cool to body temperature.

Put a quarter of the pastry aside to form the pie lid. Line the pie tin with the rest of it, gently pushing it up the sides. Insert the filling, trying not to leave any holes.

On a heavily floured surface roll out the lid and place on top of the pie. Press the lid firmly down round the edges and decorate the top with pastry shapes.

Bake in the oven at 150C/gas 2 for two hours. Allow to cool, then place in the fridge overnight.

My Mum's Lancashire Hotpot

A hotpot traditionally was that, a stew made in a tall terracotta pot. Really, any not-too-wide casserole is fine for this dish, which is synonymous with economic Lancashire working class cookery.

Note that I'm using lamb neck chops. Best end are too lean for a one-pot meal that needs a good quota of fat. The lamb's kidneys supply their own succulence. Remember to uncover the potato top layer in the final stages of cooking, so it goes crispy. Pickled red cabbage is the traditional accompaniment.

Ingredients

900g lamb neck chops

2tbsp rapeseed oil

6 lamb's kidneys, trimmed

2 large onions, sliced

1 large carrot, diced

25g flour

640ml lamb or beef stock

1 bay leaf

1tbsp chopped thyme

900g potato slices, cut as thick as your little finger

Salt

Pepper

50g butter

1 garlic clove, crushed

Method

Pre-heat your oven. Heat half the oil in a heavy bottomed casserole. Brown the lamb chops, remove them, then brown the kidneys.

Heat the pan again with the rest of the oil and slightly brown the onion and carrot. Add the flour and garlic and mix well before adding the stock slowly, stirring all the time to avoid lumps forming.

Add the bay leaf and thyme and season with salt and pepper. Remove from the pan.

Now build up your hotpot. Place a layer of lamb in the bottom, pour on some sauce/onion mix and cover with a layer of potatoes. Then repeat, finishing with an attractive layer of potatoes.

Cover and bake at 220C/gas 7 for 1 hour 30 minutes.

Remove the cover, brush the potatoes with butter and bake again until the potatoes brown and crisp up. Serve.

Classic Rag Pudding

This mill-worker's favourite is perhaps Oldham's greatest contribution to cuisine. No need for a ceramic bowl. It utilises easily available cotton or muslin rag cloths to steam the suet pudding casing for the mince and onions. I love suet for puddings, just as I love what lard gives to pastry. Mushy peas are the classic accompaniment to rag pudding. It's poor folk's food with no herbs or spices – and it's delicious. You can't "deconstruct" this kind of dish – or hotpot. They are perfect just as they are.

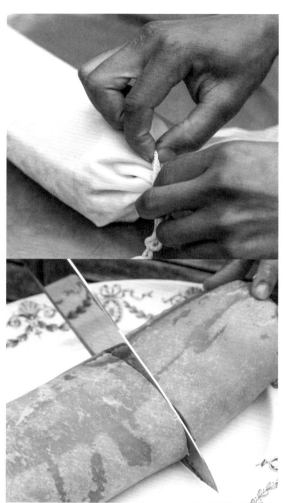

Ingredients

3tbsp rapeseed oil

450g good minced beef

1 large onion, finely chopped

1 large carrot, diced

30g plain flour

200ml good beef stock

400g suet

375g self-raising flour

30g butter

Salt and pepper

Method

Heat the oil in a heavy bottomed saucepan, brown the mince rapidly then remove from the pan. Cook the onion and carrot in the same pan until soft and the onion is translucent. Also remove. Add the butter to the pan and allow to melt and brown a little. Add the plain flour and beat together with the butter, cooking to a nice brown colour. Add the stock, stirring all the time.

Now return the meat to the pan and cook gently until all the liquid is absorbed. Remove from the heat, season and chill.

Place the suet and flour with a good pinch of salt in a bowl. Add about 6tbsp of water and mix to form a dough. Roll out this dough in a rectangle shape, about the size of two A4 sheets of paper.

Spread your meat across this, then roll up the pastry. Roll in a cotton cloth, tied at each end and steam for three hours. Serve with mushy peas and gravy.

YOU ARE OFFAL
Variety meats & old-fashioned treats

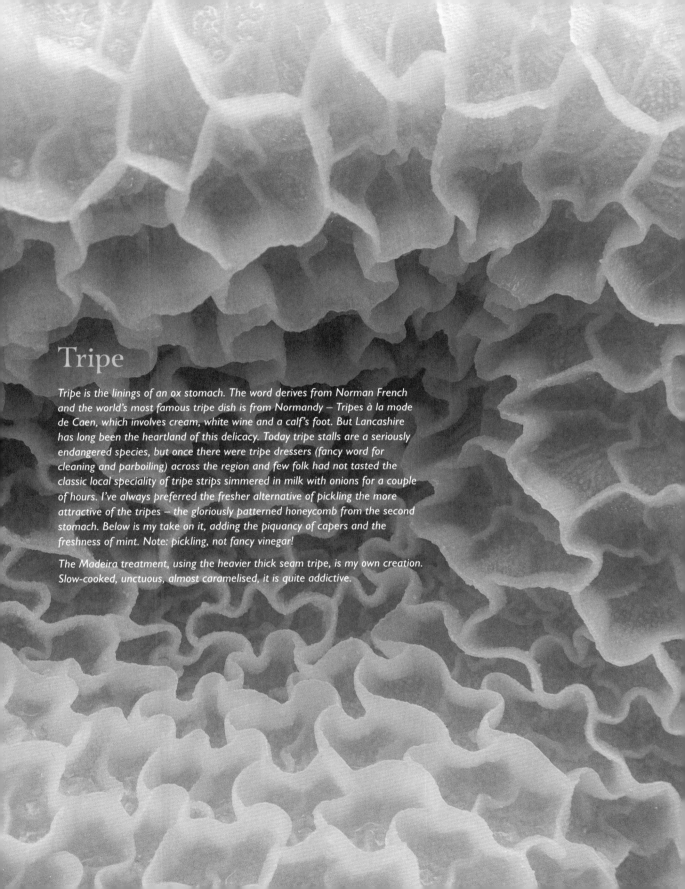

Tripe

Tripe is the linings of an ox stomach. The word derives from Norman French and the world's most famous tripe dish is from Normandy – Tripes à la mode de Caen, which involves cream, white wine and a calf's foot. But Lancashire has long been the heartland of this delicacy. Today tripe stalls are a seriously endangered species, but once there were tripe dressers (fancy word for cleaning and parboiling) across the region and few folk had not tasted the classic local speciality of tripe strips simmered in milk with onions for a couple of hours. I've always preferred the fresher alternative of pickling the more attractive of the tripes – the gloriously patterned honeycomb from the second stomach. Below is my take on it, adding the piquancy of capers and the freshness of mint. Note: pickling, not fancy vinegar!

The Madeira treatment, using the heavier thick seam tripe, is my own creation. Slow-cooked, unctuous, almost caramelised, it is quite addictive.

Pickled Tripe

Ingredients

300g honeycomb tripe

2 shallots, thinly sliced

50g chopped capers

50g garden mint, finely shredded

250ml clear pickling vinegar

Pinch coarse salt

Pinch coarse black pepper

Method

Cut the tripe into strips the size of your little finger and place in a clean stainless steel bowl.

Add the shallots, capers and seasoning. Pour on the vinegar and toss gently to ensure the tripe is fully coated. Cover and refrigerate for 12 hours.

Remove from the fridge, add the fresh mint and toss gently. Serve immediately with crusty brown bread and maybe a little butter.

Madeira Tripe

Ingredients

- 500g thick seam tripe, sliced as thick as your finger
- 500g onions, sliced
- 30g salted butter
- 30g plain flour
- 175ml Madeira
- Pinch salt and pepper
- 300ml brown stock ((or substitute with a good shop-bought beef stock)
- 1tsp tomato puree
- 1 bay leaf

Method

Heat an ovenproof heavy bottomed pan. Add the onions, bay leaf and butter. Cook until golden brown. Add the flour and tomato puree and beat until there are no lumps. Add the tripe, Madeira and stock. Season.

Cover and cook at 140C/gas 1 for two hours. Uncover and reduce until thick and sticky. Season and serve on thick slices of toast or mashed potatoes.

Duck Liver and Black Pudding Terrine

I have been quite restrained in my use of black pudding in these recipes but couldn't resist marrying it here with succulent duck liver to make an uncomplicated but classic terrine. Don't forget to use one of the black puddings with little cubes of pure pork fat to ensure the right fatty texture. This is lovely with some caramelised onion relish.

Ingredients

200g duck fat

1 medium onion, finely chopped

1tsp chopped thyme

Salt and pepper

200g fatty black pudding, skinned

600g trimmed, de-veined duck livers

25ml good brandy

25ml rapeseed oil

Method

Heat the oil and cook the onion and thyme gently until soft and translucent. Set aside.

Heat the duck fat in a large, heavy frying pan until it starts to smoke. Add the livers (you could use chicken at a pinch) and cook until just pink inside. Add the brandy and set alight.

Transfer the livers and onions to a blender and work until smooth. Season to taste.

Fold the black pudding through the liver mix, pack into a terrine mould and set in the fridge for 12 hours. Turn out and slice.

Crispy Ox Tongue with Mustard Mayonnaise

Tongues often come salted and pickled. I get mine raw. You just have to to boil them and boil them until they are tender, allow to cool and then peel off the unappetising looking grey skin and gristle. If this is too much for you, this dish does work with tinned tongue. Deep-fried in breadcrumbs with a piquant dip, it makes lovely finger food, beefily rich.

Ingredients

500ml water

1 ox tongue

1500ml beef stock

1 carrot

1 leek

1 onion

1 stick celery

Salt and pepper

2 bay leaves

2 eggs

300g breadcrumbs

100ml milk

300g plain flour

Method

Place the tongue in a large stock pan, add the vegetables, bay leaves, stock, water, salt and pepper.

Bring to the boil, then turn down to a simmer for two hours. Keep skimming the foam from the top.

Remove the tongue and chill. When the tongue gets to body temperature peel the skin off, then chill till cold. Beat the eggs and milk together.

Cut the tongue into index finger sized strips. Roll them in the flour, then the egg and finally the breadcrumbs.

Deep fry in hot oil and serve immediately with mustard mayonnaise (powdered mustard stirred into bought-in mayo, to taste, is fine).

Braised Lamb Hearts

Ox hearts are probably too big and tough to tackle for most people, but I'm not averse to flash-frying wafer-thin slices of the stuff. Delicious. Still, the hearts of pigs and sheep are more manageable and make better eating. Your butcher is unlikely to parade them in the front of his cool counter, but he can certainly supply them. Get him to trim away the fat and all the veins and arteries and you'll find the heart's cavity is perfect for stuffing. This is definitely a cut that benefits from a good, long braise, though.

Ingredients

4 lamb hearts, tubes trimmed

2 crushed garlic cloves

8 rashers of streaky bacon, minced

2 large onions, finely chopped

Salt

Pepper

200g sausage meat, uncooked

50g breadcrumbs

50g butter

1 bay leaf

25g plain flour

1tbsp tomato puree

200ml red wine

1tbsp chopped parsley

1tbsp chopped tarragon

1tbsp rapeseed oil

Method

First make the stuffing. Heat half the butter in a saucepan, add the bacon and half the onion and cook gently until the onion is soft but without colour. Add a pinch of pepper and the breadcrumbs. Beat together and remove from heat, then stir in the sausage meat thoroughly. Fill the hearts with your stuffing, squishing it in firmly. Set aside in the fridge. Use any leftover stuffing as little dumplings. Simply roll into balls and fry.

For the sauce: Heat the rapeseed oil in a saucepan, slightly brown the remaining onions and add the garlic. Mix in the flour and the tomato puree. Now beat in the stock, a little at a time to avoid any lumps and beat in the wine. Set the sauce aside.

Heat a heavy casserole dish and oil and brown the hearts. Pour over the sauce and cover. Bake for 2 hours 30 minutes at 220C/gas 7. Remove the cover, stir in the parsley and tarragon, season and serve.

Devilled Rabbit Kidneys and Livers on Toast

A toothsome rich snack from the parts of the rabbit you might be tempted to discard. Don't! You have to be quick with this as the offal will over-cook in seconds and taste rather bitter and rubbery. I make up the sauce before I cook it.

Ingredients

4 slices of toast made from thickly sliced granary bread

25g unsalted butter

8 trimmed rabbit livers

16 rabbit kidneys

1tbsp chopped parsley

2 finely chopped shallots

A good pinch of cayenne pepper

Salt and pepper

1tbsp English mustard

10ml double cream

3tbsp rapeseed oil

1tsp redcurrant jelly

100ml sherry

Method

Heat 1tbsp of the oil in a small saucepan. Add shallot and cayenne pepper and cook until the shallot softens.

Add the sherry and reduce by half, then the redcurrant jelly and mustard.

Stir in the double cream and remove from the heat.

Warm up a heavy frying pan and add the rest of the oil. Put in livers and kidneys. Brown rapidly. Pour the sauce over and mix quickly. Add parsley, season and serve immediately.

Head Cheese (or Brawn)

Prep-wise it's perhaps not a dish for the faint-hearted, but it's worth being brave. The results are lovely. Strictly speaking, head cheese uses just minced pork; brawn shredded chunks, including the delicious cheeks. The meat in this dish, which dates back centuries, can come from both shoulder and head, but head's enough. A clean-shaven head! You need to remove the hairs, so it's important to shave the pig. No one wants wiry pig hairs in their meal. Use a disposable razor or a blowtorch, paying particular attention to the insides of the ears. If you've got this far, you are definitely ready to make brawn.

The natural jelly in the head bones should be enough to set the brawn. End product is a glistening mosaic of flesh and veg best served cold, naturally.

Ingredients

1 pig's head (best if it's split. Get your butcher to do this.)

12 juniper berries

12 peppercorns

3 bay leaves

2 onions, roughly chopped

2 carrots, roughly chopped

1 stick celery, roughly chopped

2tsp salt

2tsp chopped parsley

Method

Take a large stock pan and lay your veg on the bottom. Add the salt, peppercorns and juniper berries. Stick your halved pigs' heads on top so that they are looking up at you. Cover with water and bring to the boil.

As soon as the pan boils, turn it down and simmer for three hours, skimming frequently while cooking.

Gently remove the heads from the pan and set aside. Strain the liquid and reduce to 400ml, skimming all the time. Pick all the flesh from the head, including the tongue, and dice into 1cm pieces.

Place the meat and chopped parsley into a bowl, season and add enough cooking liquor to moisten and evenly coat the meat. Pack into a tin lined with greaseproof or cling film (it makes it easier to lift out) and refrigerate for 12 hours.

Slice and serve. Lovely with pickles, mustard or a watercress salad.

CHEESY & EGGY
Simple farmyard delights

Lancashire Rarebit

Kirkham's is synonymous with traditional Lancashire cheese. On their Goosnargh farm, the family mix the curd from three days' milk, using very little starter, so the acidity rises more slowly, allowing the natural flora of the milk to develop their full flavour. All their cheeses are rich and buttery, perfect for melting and sauces... while on a toasted crumpet Lancashire makes the perfect rarebit.

Ingredients

25g butter

25g flour

200ml milk

1tbsp English mustard

1tsp Worcester sauce

2 large free range eggs, separated

100g crumbly Lancashire cheese (Mrs Kirkham's Tasty is best)

Crumpets

Freshly milled pepper

Method

Melt the butter in a small saucepan, blend in the flour and cook for two minutes. Slowly add the milk and blend thoroughly for two minutes.

Take the pan off the heat and blend in the mustard and Worcester sauce. Now blend in the egg yolks and place to one side to cool before blending in the cheese. Toast the crumpets on one side.

Whisk the egg whites until stiff and, using a metal spoon, carefully fold the egg whites into the cheese mixture. Cover the crumpets with this. Grill until golden brown.

Lancashire Omelette

An interesting take on the perfect high-fat hangover cure or a great hearty lunch. The fat hit of the cheese, black pudding and bacon is matched by the duck eggs. I use a lot of duck eggs, as you'll see in the following recipes. They fell out of fashion after the Second World War because of salmonella fears and the rise of chicken-based factory egg production, but are making a comeback. The yolks are larger and higher in fat than a hen's egg, which makes them richer. They're also packed with vitamins, minerals and protein.

Ingredients

3 duck eggs

1 spring onion, finely chopped

80g grated Mrs Kirkham's Lancashire

Half a black pudding link, diced

2 rashers of bacon, chopped

Salt (use sparingly) and pepper

2tbsp rapeseed oil

Method

Beat the eggs, then heat the oil in a heavy bottomed non-stick pan.

Fry the bacon and black pudding. Add the spring onion and cook a further 30 seconds.

Pour on the egg, sprinkle over the cheese and bake in a very hot oven for six minutes.

Duck Egg Omelette "Arnold Bennett Style"

Arnold Bennett (1867-1931) is better known these days for the omelette named after him rather than his writings. The Savoy Hotel created this dish of egg, smoked haddock and parmesan in his honour and he was so delighted, he demanded it on every visit. Omelette Arnold Bennett is still on the menu at The Savoy. Mine is a lighter variant on the classic.

Ingredients

3 duck eggs

30g good Cheddar, grated

60g cream cheese

60g natural smoked haddock, sliced thinly

30g chopped chives

½tsp English mustard

15g butter

Pinch salt and pepper

Method

Preheat your oven to 240C/gas 9.

Beat the duck eggs, chives, cream cheese and mustard together.

Heat an oven-proof omelette pan, add butter and allow to foam before pouring in the egg mix. Next add the haddock and grated cheese. Bake for four minutes or until set.

Crispy Lancashire Black Pudding Potato Cake topped with a Softly Poached Duck Egg and a Tarragon Mustard Mayonnaise

This dish dates back to my days at the stove in Mr Thomas's Chop House. It's so loved by my customers, I can never take it off the menu. Like so many Chop House stalwarts from those days, it's hearty fare. You want to mop up every last morsel from your plate.

Ingredients

375g black pudding, skin removed

225g potato boiled and mashed with butter

1 free range egg yolk

50g seasoned flour

2 free range eggs, whisked with a little milk

100g fresh breadcrumbs

Cooking oil

4 duck eggs, softly poached

15ml fresh tarragon

15ml black mustard seeds

15ml English mustard

150ml thick mayonnaise

225g rocket or watercress

Freshly milled black pepper

Method

Thoroughly stir together the black pudding, mashed potato and egg yolk. It should be lumpy rather than smooth. Divide the mixture into four and with floured hands shape into cakes 5cm deep and 15cm in diameter.

Dip into the beaten egg, then coat generously with breadcrumbs.

Heat the oil in a frying pan and fry until the cakes are golden brown on both sides. Keep warm in the oven. Meanwhile poach the duck eggs and keep warm.

Put the tarragon, mustard seed and mustard into a bowl and blend thoroughly with the mayonnaise.

Place a little rocket or watercress on each plate, top with a black pudding potato cake and poached egg. Sprinkle the mayonnaise over the top. Finish with freshly milled pepper.

You could also deep fry the cakes at 170C for six minutes.

Coddled Duck Eggs with Port of Lancaster Smoked Haddock and Chives

More duck eggs and smoked haddock (from the outstanding Port of Lancaster operation), but I'm unrepentant. What could be better than creamy, substantial snacks like these, paired with a pint of real ale. We usually have six on draught at the Mark Addy, including our own hoppy Fearless brew, made for us by RedWillow of Macclesfield.

Ingredients

2tbsp butter

4 large duck eggs

150g finely chopped smoked haddock

160ml double cream

1tbsp chopped chives

Salt

Pepper

Pinch of paprika

Method

Mix the haddock and half the cream together, fold in the chives and season with paprika, salt and pepper.

Spoon the fish mixture into ramekins and top with the duck egg, being careful not to break the yolk.

Pour on the remaining cream and bake in a bain-marie for six to seven minutes. (A bain-marie is a double boiler, where one pan is placed inside another containing water at simmering point, surrounding the food with a very gentle heat.)

This dish is lovely with granary toast.

LIVING ON THE VEG
Meat-free & marvellous

Chilled Pea and Mint Soup

A perfect summery soup, one of the dishes I created for the Manchester International Festival's groundbreaking Biospheric Project, which championed "urban farming". If you are not a vegetarian feel free to add a rasher of bacon to cook with the onion and garlic!

Ingredients

1tbsp rapeseed oil

1 large onion, diced

2 cloves garlic, peeled and chopped

500ml vegetable stock

675g shelled fresh (or frozen) peas

1 round lettuce, washed and chopped

Salt

Freshly ground white pepper

4tbsp sour cream

Fresh mint sprigs for garnish

Method

Heat the oil in a large pan. Add the spring onions and garlic and gently cook for five to seven minutes – or until the onion is soft but not brown.

Pour in the stock and bring to the boil. Add the peas, bring back to the boil and reduce to the simmering point before stirring in the lettuce and mint. Cook for a further two minutes until the peas are tender.

Blend the slightly cooled soup mixture, using a liquidiser or hand blender, until smooth. Season, then pour into a large bowl and allow to cool. Cover and chill for four hours or preferably overnight.

To serve, spoon the soup into chilled bowls. Scoop 1tbsp of cream into each soup helping and top with a mint sprig.

Wild Garlic Tart

I love the freshness of wild garlic, its sheer abundance, its oh-so-brief season and the unmistakeable delicate fragrance it gives to the countryside. It grows all along the upper Irwell Valley. It is the smell I remember best from my childhood. As soon as I see a patch I can't help but fill my pockets full of the stuff. Like nettles, it makes great soup; with crushed walnuts a powerful pesto; and this exquisite, creamy tart.

Ingredients

450g shortcrust pastry

Pinch salt

80ml double cream

6 large eggs

200g cream cheese

300g wild garlic

50g grated Cheddar

½ tsp nutmeg

Salt and pepper

Method

Line a 30cm quiche tin with pastry and blind bake the crust.

Plunge your wild garlic into a large, heavy-bottomed pan of boiling water, remove after 10 seconds and cool in iced water.

Squeeze as much water as you can from the wild garlic and finely chop it.

Beat together the eggs, nutmeg, cream cheese, pinch of salt, pinch of pepper and double cream. Mix in the wild garlic and pour into the tart case. Sprinkle with the Cheddar and bake for 30 minutes at 200C/gas 6.

Really nice warm with a dollop of mint-flecked natural yoghurt.

Globe Artichokes With Curried Mayonnaise

Glorified thistles they may be, but globe artichokes are a top vegetable treat. It's not just the hearts. Scraping the flesh from the choke tips and dipping in a spicy mayonnaise like the one below is great, messy fun.

Ingredients

2 lemons, 1 juiced, 1 halved

4 globe artichokes, stalks removed

2 egg yolks

1tsp curry powder

1tbsp lime juice

1 pinch cayenne pepper

100g coriander, finely chopped

25ml groundnut oil

1tsp Dijon mustard

Method

To make the mayonnaise, clean the mixing bowl, add the egg yolks, mustard, cayenne, curry powder and combine. Whisk in the nut oil very slowly in one continuous drizzle. Fold in the rest of the ingredients and chill, ready to serve.

Bring a large pan of salted water to the boil, add the lemon halves.

Drop in the chokes and boil for 30 minutes. Serve immediately.

Pearl Barley Risotto with Beetroot and Leagram's Curd Cheese

Leagram Organic Dairy of Chipping produce amazing quality curd cheeses, from goat's and ewe's milk, that many of the country's leading chefs use. Barley is, in my opinion, far better than risotto rice. It has a lovely mouthfeel. As it's grown in the UK, it's got to be more sustainable. Spelt is an interesting alternative, too. It's an ancient species of wheat that's now readily available.

Ingredients

2 garlic cloves, crushed

4tbsp rapeseed oil

300g curd cheese

1large onion, finely chopped

300g pearl barley

200g cooked, diced beetroot

1tsp chopped thyme

700ml vegetable stock

25g butter

4tbsp mascarpone

Salt and black pepper

100g baby leaf spinach

20g chopped chives

Method

Bake the beetroot in its skin in foil; much better than boiling. When cool, skin and dice.

Heat the oil in a heavy bottomed saucepan. Add the garlic, thyme and onion and cook gently until the onion is soft, without colouring it. Include the butter, barley and stock and simmer for 30 minutes, stirring occasionally. You may have to add extra stock before the barley is cooked, but you need the grain to have a little bite to it.

Once cooked, fold in the beetroot, spinach, mascarpone, cheese and chives. Season and serve immediately.

Shropshire Blue Cheese Onion Bhajis with Dandelion and Burdock Syrup

The heavily reduced pop syrup and the blue cheese in the bhajis makes a piquant veggie snack combo.

Ingredients

2 eggs

3 medium onions, sliced

120g plain flour

½ tsp ground cumin

250g Shropshire Blue (or pick your own favourite blue)

500ml dandelion and burdock

Method

Place the fizzy pop in a big pan and boil it down until it reduces by 90 per cent. Set this aside.

In a bowl combine the eggs, onion, cheese, cumin and flour. Mix in the onions until they are evenly coated. Divide the mixture into four patties and spoon them into hot fat (about 160C/gas 3). Fry for two minutes and then turn them over.

Drain the bhajis, season and dribble with the dandelion and burdock syrup.

SWEET SENSATIONS
Sticky, crumbly and creamy

Eccles Cake Served with a Dollop of Mrs Dowsons Clotted Cream

A glossy golden disc of flaky pastry filled with rich fruit, sugar and spice – total, sensual delight. You can understand how the Puritans, after banning dancing on the Village Green at Eccles, also prohibited the eating of cakes at religious festivals. Eccles folk went on baking and eating them undercover. Witness an old local song celebrating fairs and wakes: "With music and cakes for to keep up the wakes among wenches and fine country beaux."

Tradition traces Eccles Cakes to Mrs Elizabeth Raffald, whose influential cookery book, 'The Experienced English Housekeeper' of 1786 had a recipe for 'sweet patties'. But her version included boiled calf's foot, apples, oranges, nutmeg, egg yolk, currants and brandy and could be baked or fried. Quite different.

The amazing Mrs Raffald, who went from housekeeper at Arley Hall to running a recruitment agency in Manchester while bearing 16 children (all daughters), is a personal hero of mine and her book is still an essential source for anyone interested in the roots of our regional cuisine.

By the 19th century two shops in the town kept the Eccles Cake tradition alive. Wardles and The Old Original Eccles Cake Shop are now as long gone as Eccles Village Green. I like to feel the Mark Addy honours their sugary, spicy legacy. Pass the clotted cream.

Ingredients

40g soft butter

100g caster sugar

200g currants

Pinch nutmeg

50g candied peel

Pinch ground ginger

500g puff pastry dough

Mrs Dowsons clotted cream, to serve

Method

Combine the butter, sugar, fruit and spice.

Roll out the pastry to about 4mm thick and cut it into 10cm circles

Place a small spoonful of filling into the centre of each circle. Draw the edges together over the fruit and pinch to seal. Then turn over and press gently to flatten the cakes.

Make a small slash in the top of each cake and place on a baking sheet.

Brush with a little water and lightly dust with sugar before baking for about 20 minutes at 220C/gas 7. Allow to cool and serve with the cream.

Simple Caramelised Rhubarb Tart with Clotted Cream

A variant on Tarte Tatin, so be careful when tipping the tart upside down. Ideally use four small shallow pans with handles, otherwise use one larger size, though it can be more unwieldy to tip. We are dealing with hot, hot sugar here and it can bite. It's so far removed from my experience of rhubarb as a child, which mainly focused around a stick from the patch and a bag of Silver Spoon sugar. We are blessed in the North with a fine rhubarb history – early great croppers like Timperley and fine men and women who treat the cultivation of the stuff like a religion.

Ingredients

300g puff pastry

4 stalks of rhubarb, thicker the better, 1 per person

125g caster sugar

150g butter

2 vanilla pods, each cut into four

200g clotted cream

Method

Pre-heat the oven to 200C/gas 6.

Roll out the pastry 4mm thick and cut into four discs slightly larger than the pans. Dock the pastry (ie pincushion it with small holes) and chill it.

Heat the pans and divide the butter into them. Allow the butter to foam slightly, then sprinkle the sugar on to the butter. Add the rhubarb – I normally fill an individual pan with four pieces, cut just shy of the diameter of the pastry disc – and cook steadily until the sugar starts to caramelise. Now add a piece of vanilla pod to each pan.

Place the pastry discs on top of the rhubarb, keeping the pastry tucked down the inside of the pans.

Bake for 25 to 30 minutes or until the pastry is golden brown. Very carefully tip the pan upside down onto a plate, top with clotted cream and serve immediately.

Handmade Chocolate Mousse

There's only one way to make chocolate mousse – with your hands. It's one of the great sensual experiences. When Manchester life coach and author Thea Euryphaessa approached me to host a Sensual Eating event at The Mark Addy, I happily agreed and chocolate was a delectable part of the syllabus. In Thea's enthusiastic words: "You could have a lot of fun with this recipe. Yeah, sure, you can stick it in Martini glasses, dust it with some icing sugar, make it all look glamorous. Alternatively, you could smear it all over someone." Not the usual reaction to a Mark Addy dish.

Ingredients

100g of good honey (needs to be runny and from happy, horny bees – ours was from the Salford Bee Collective)

300g rich dark chocolate

550ml of double cream

Method

Gently melt the chocolate in a double boiler saucepan.

In a spotlessly clean bowl, whip the double cream until it forms soft peaks.

Wash your hands. Drizzle the honey over the cream, then fold together the chocolate, cream and honey with your hands.

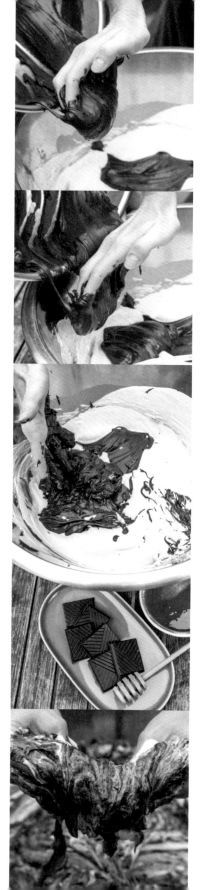

Filbert Nut Brittle

A sweet snack, simple and fun, this makes a gorgeous garnish for ice cream. Filberts are young, "green" hazelnuts, not dried.

Ingredients

300g filberts
250g caster sugar
100ml water

Method

Shell your filberts, then bake them at 190C/gas 5 for 10 minutes or less. You want them golden brown, no more.

Take a heavy-bottomed pan – it needs to be spotless otherwise your sugar may crystallize – add the sugar and water and boil. You are looking for an even brown colour. Take care, it's so very hot. Add the nuts, remove the pan from the heat and wobble or shake it to cover all the nuts.

Pour the mix on to a slightly oiled sheet of greaseproof paper. Allow to set, then break it up… and eat it. Simple.

Elderberry (or Gooseberry) Fool with Lemon Balm Wafers

OK, the lemon balm is more about scent than taste, but the colour is nice and it helps. Elderberries are not commercially grown but can easily be found in the wild. Pick the heads of the berries and be sure to wash and cook them thoroughly before using – raw elderberries contain a poisonous alkaloid but become harmless when cooked. Always remove their stalks, though. Gooseberries are a fine alternative.

Ingredients

250g elderberries or gooseberries, topped & tailed

50g honey

2tbsp water

200g thick yoghurt

2tbsp icing sugar

Quarter of a vanilla pod, split and scraped

200ml double cream

For the lemon balm wafers:

120g flour

80ml lemon juice

Finely grated zest of 1 lemon

250g caster sugar

100g melted unsalted butter

200g ground almonds

25g lemon balm, finely shredded

50ml limoncello

Method

To make the wafers: Beat all the ingredients together with the exception of the lemon balm. Only fold that in when the mixture is smooth.

Place a teaspoonful of wafer mix on to a large non-stick baking tray and, with moistened fingers, spread as thin as you can. The mix is going to further spread three times as much, so do not over-fill the tray.

Bake at 180C/gas 4 until golden brown. Remove from tray and cool.

To make the fool: Heat the honey, water and gooseberries together gently until the fruit starts to fall apart.

Remove from the heat and pass the whole lot together through a fine sieve. Set the pulp aside in the fridge.

Beat together the yoghurt vanilla and icing sugar. Slowly pour in the cream, whisking all the time (but do not over-whisk). Fold in the gooseberry mixture.

Place in serving glasses, chill for an hour, then top with the wafers and serve.

Banana and Salford Honey Pudding

Steamy, rich and maybe a little stick-to-your ribs but lovely all the same. The Salford honey is fantastic and for the historically minded, Salford Docks was one of the largest import centres for bananas in the world.

Ingredients

100g unsalted butter, softened

100g caster sugar

200g bananas (a little over-ripe's fine, too ripe and your pud will be an unappealing grey)

¼tsp grated nutmeg

2 large eggs, beaten

160g self-raising flour

6tbsp honey

Method

Cream the butter and sugar together with 2tbsp of honey until pale and smooth and you can feel the sugar crystals. Then beat in your banana and nutmeg.

Slowly beat in your eggs, a little at a time, before folding in the sifted flour.

Grease four ramekins. Pour 1tbsp of honey in each, followed by the mix. Be sure to fill them only three quarters the way up. Cover with cling film and steam for 30 minutes.

Turn out and serve with cream or custard.

Benedictine Cambridge Creams

The French lay a strong claim to inventing this classic vanilla custard with a hardened sugar crust, which they call crème brûlée. It first appears in a celebrated French cook book at the end of the 17th century, but a variant of this pudding had already featured for 60 years on the menu at Trinity College, Cambridge (it's also known as Trinity Cream).

In flavouring my version with Benedictine, I'm not so much kowtowing to the French as honouring those Lancashire lads – the Accrington Pals – who crossed the Channel to fight in the Great War and acquired a taste for this herbal, Cognac-based liqueur, mixing it with hot water. Today Burnley Miners Club is still the world's biggest consumer of Benedictine; Burnley FC sell it on matchdays.

Ingredients

250ml double cream

150ml milk

1 vanilla pod, split and scraped

4 egg yolks

40g caster sugar

100ml Benedictine

70g raisins

Method

Marinate the raisins in the Benedictine in a small, covered container for 24 hours.

Gently bring to a simmer the milk, cream, vanilla pod and seeds with the Benedictine from the raisins.

Beat the egg yolks and sugar together until smooth.

Strain the milk and cream mix to remove the pod and pour gently on to the eggs, beating all the time.

Pour the mix into four greased ramekins, then drop the raisins in. Bake in a bain marie in the oven at 150C/gas 2 for 30 minutes or until just set. Remove and refrigerate until cold.

Before serving, caramelise the top by using a thin layer of sugar. A blow torch gives the best result, or you can flash it under the grill.

Celebrations Terrine

Indulge your inner child. This is a souped-up version of the chocolate crispy cake, made from the Mars selection box, Celebrations, a mixture of mini-versions of chocolate favourites Mars, Bounty, Snickers, Galaxy, Topic, Twix, Milky Way and more.

Ingredients

600g dark chocolate

400g of your choice of Celebrations bars, whole

225ml double cream

320g unsalted butter, melted

6 egg yolks

100g icing sugar

60ml Tia Maria

Method

Place the chocolate and cream into a mixing bowl over simmering water (don't allow the bowl to touch), beating until they combine, then beat in the butter, too. Move to a warm place.

Place a new clean bowl over the water, add the Tia Maria, sugar and egg yolks. Whisk until they thicken a little, so your whisk leaves a trail.

Now whisk your egg mix into your chocolate mix and fold in the Celebrations. Pour into a lined terrine mould and chill for 12 hours.

Vimto Trifle

I like Vimto – the iconic drink that was created in the North West and conquered the world. I like trifle, too. I like big trifles in big bowls that squelch when you dig into them with a spoon. The custard's a bit of a cheat. Accompany with Goosnargh cakes – glorified shortbread with caraway – and it's just perfect.

Ingredients

300ml hot Vimto, made as strong as you like

6 leaves of gelatine

200g spongy fingers

100g raspberries

100g blackberries

700ml double cream

4 egg yolks

1 vanilla pod, split, scraped

30g caster sugar

1tsp cornflour

50g flaked almonds, toasted, as an optional flourish

Method

Soak the leaf gelatine until soft, then drain and dissolve in warm Vimto.

Place the sponge fingers in your bowl, sprinkle on the fruit, then pour on the Vimto. Chill it.

Make the custard by heating 300ml of cream and vanilla to just below a simmer. Whisk the sugar, cornflour and eggs together in a bowl. Pour on the hot cream and whisk again.

Return to the pan and stir slowly over a low heat until it thickens. Too hot and your egg will scramble!

Allow to cool, then pour into the jelly. Chill again in the fridge.

Whip your cream, adding a little sugar and vanilla if you like then pipe on the cream. Sprinkle with almonds.

INDEX

A

B

C

D

H

I

K

W

Y

THANKS

Mum and Dad for shoving me along
Michelle
Wayne Rosenfield from Styal Meats
Rob Poole of Poole's Produce
Steve and Ric from Chef Direct
Phil, my sous chef (couldn't have done it without you, lad}
All the gang at the Addy; especially owner Margaret Hope, our guiding light
And, of course, all our loyal customers

Thanks, too, to all who allowed us on their territory for the photoshoots:
Graham Salt, skipper of the Princess Catherine
Sarah and Manchester Clay Shooting Club
Wayne at Styal Meats
Andrew at The Real Lancashire Black Pudding Company in Haslingden
Faye at Leagram Organic Dairy up at Chipping in the Ribble Valley
Biospheric Project in Irwell House, Salford
Dom and Chris at Fitzpatrick's Temperance Bar in Rawtenstall

And finally, thanks to three gents who made this book happen:
Mr Sowerby, writer and editor
Mr Catto, photographer and designer
Mr Schofield, publisher